African Traditional Religion and Christian Counseling

Karl Grebe and Wilfred Fon

InSIGHT BOOKS
AFRICAN ISSUES
AFRICA'S AUTHORS

OASIS

African Traditional Religion and Christian Counseling

Karl Grebe and Wilfred Fon

Karl Grebe
Mile 3 Nkwen
P.O. Box 5025
Bamenda - Nkwen
Cameroon

African Traditional Religion
By Karl H. Grebe and Rev. Dr. Wilford Fon

Copyright © 2006 **Oasis International Ltd.**

First edition 1995. Second edition 1997 copyright © Karl Grebe.

Oasis International Limited exists to meet the unique needs of English speaking Africa,
Asia and the Caribbean. Oasis works to produce literature that is both relevant and affordable.
For information contact **Oasis International Ltd: info@oasisint.net.**

Cover design by Robyn Martins

ISBN: 978-1-59452-075-4

Printed in India

Table of Contents

A Word about the Authors

KARL H. GREBE is a member of the Summer Institute of Linguistics (SIL). He and his wife, Winnie, are Canadians who have been working with SIL in Cameroon since 1971. Karl is a graduate of Briercrest Bible College in Canada and has an MA in Linguistics from the University of Calgary. For the last few years he has been serving in Cameroon as a Bible translation consultant, based at the SIL Regional Office in Bamenda, the capital of North West Province. Earlier he did linguistic research on Lam Nso', the language of the Nso' people, and oversaw the translation of the New Testament into this language. Karl and Winnie have two adults sons who are married and living in Canada.

WILFRED T.W. FON is the President of the Cameroon Baptist Theological Seminary in Ndu, North West Province of Cameroon. He received his B.Th. from the same seminary as a member of the first graduating class in 1988. Later, he did further studies in the USA where he received an M.Th. from Bethel Theological Seminary in Minneapolis, and a Ph.D. from Westminster Theological Seminary in Philadelphia. Wilfred is an ordained pastor of the Cameroon Baptist Convention and had served as a pastor for several years before embarking on his academic and teaching career. Dr. Fon and his wife, Angelica, have four children and make their home at the seminary in Ndu.

Preface

The beginnings of this booklet go back into the mid seventies when I was working with the Nso' people in the NW Province of Cameroon to develop the written form of their language and to translate the New Testament into it. Having learned to speak Lamnso', and living with the people in a traditional compound, I was very much aware that the spirit world is an ever present reality in people's lives to the extent that much of what happens in the seen world is believed to originate from the unseen world.

Life in the extended family is intricately intertwined with rituals of relating to the spirits of the departed who are seen to be the real guardians of the family. Gods and nature spirits live in the land. Some are revered; others are feared. The world is filled with mystical powers that people can tap into for the use of magic, charms, divination, self advancement and witchcraft. Some people are born with the ability to move in the spirit world and harness its powers. Others acquire this ability by initiation. The majority relies on the services of a host of specialists from the family priest to diviners, sorcerers, witch doctors, fetish specialists and spiritual healers. Their services are in constant demand because life is precarious and real power rests in the spirit world. God is seen as the Creator of the seen and the unseen world. He placed man into this world, expecting him to work out his destiny by using all the powers he has provided.

I soon realized that this view of the world is not unique to the traditional Nso' person but is largely shared by the Christians as well. This is evidenced by the fact that in crises Christians often revert to the same practices as the traditionalist because these alone are believed to be truly effective. For many, Christ is seen as the Savior for eternal life to come in heaven. He has little to do with the practical problems of this life. In this life one has to help oneself using whatever works, because God is believed to have provided all these means.

As we were translating the first portions of the New Testament into Lamnso' the translators needed to decide on what Lamnso' terms to use for translating such biblical terms as angel, devil, demon and the various activities of demons or evil spirits. So I organized a workshop for Christian leaders in which we sketched the way the Nso' people traditionally view the spirit world and attempted to relate this to the view of the spirit world as revealed in the Bible. We soon found that even the most experienced Christian leaders were not always sure how to relate the cultural phenomena to the biblical picture. On the whole, the church had bypassed the task of interpreting the cultural picture from the biblical per-

7

spective, leaving Christians to determine for themselves how to relate to the various traditions of their culture. The Lamnso' term the churches had traditionally used for demon means literally "evil breath". This is a literal translation of the Greek term for evil spirit. However, it is not a name of any one of the spirit beings known to the Nso' traditionally. As a result, the biblical accounts about demons and their activities did not connect with the experiences of the Nso' people in their daily world in which they deal with different spirit phenomena. During the workshop a cultural term for demon was proposed. This term was tested over several years and found to be much more relevant. It was then used in the final draft of the New Testament.

However, proper terminology alone is not sufficient. It must be accompanied by a conscious effort of the church to teach Christian discernment and to equip the Christians to live victoriously in their culture that is permeated with fear of the spirit world. This entails teaching the biblical resources for spiritual warfare and ministering to the spiritually oppressed. It was this vision for the church which I started to share whenever I was approached over the years to speak to Cameroonian Christian workers about cultural issues in evangelism or to orient new missionaries.

The impetus to put the material of these seminars into a document for wider use came in 1986, when I was asked by one of the professors of the Cameroon Baptist Theological Seminary to serve as a consultant on the development of a counseling handbook for Cameroonian pastors. A draft, prepared by a Western Christian psychologist, was available for adaptation to the local scene. This draft had no section dealing with the spirit world. To make up for this deficiency Wilfred Fon, who was then a student at the seminary, and I wrote a chapter on the African view of the spirit world and its relationship to Christian counseling. As authors we took the perspective of the Cameroonian Christian worker looking at his own worldview which explains the editorial "we" used in the article. Later, I added further sections based on new reading and on experience gained in counseling situations. Upon popular request, I finally put all this material together in the form of the present booklet which was first published in 1995.

It is my prayer, and that of Dr. Fon, that God may use this imperfect work of ours to help church leaders and Christians in Cameroon to interpret their culture from a biblical perspective and to minister more effectively to the spiritually oppressed.

Karl Grebe
Bamenda, Cameroon

1.0 The World View of African Traditional Religion

Most African Christians have grown up in cultures that are intricately intertwined with the traditional religion of that ethnic group. These indigenous African religions vary in detail but they agree in essentials such as, the spiritual nature of the world, the existence and remoteness of God, the role of spirits and mystical powers, and the way man relates to his world and to God. Furthermore, ethnographic studies have shown that in all cases the religion of African peoples is at the very heart of their cultures. It controls much of their social systems, is the main source of power, and regulates matters relating to the land and the weather on which the most Africans depend for their survival.

We can thus talk about African traditional religions or ATR as a whole, as well as about a worldview that is common to those who grew up in a culture with an ATR background. Becoming a Christian does not automatically change all of one's worldview nor does it need to change completely. Conversion is first and foremost a switch of allegiance from whatever one trusted in before to Christ and the Word of God. In the African setting this usually means forsaking the ancestor cult and all dealings with the spirit world and trusting Christ. From there follows a new purpose in life and a new way of dealing with life's problems, whatever they may be in light of the worldview of one's culture.

The Christian counselor needs to know intimately the worldview of the counselee, in order to understand his problems and temptations. Furthermore, he needs to have a clear grasp of the essentials of ATR and to have interpreted them in light of the Scriptures, so that he knows what are the strongholds of Satan in ATR that need to be broken down, and what are neutral cultural aspects, or even elements of truth that he can build on in guiding the counselee to biblical solutions. In the remainder of this section we shall attempt to outline the essentials of ATR and the worldview that results from it.

1.1 The Spiritual Nature of the World

In the everyday life of our African cultures we are constantly aware of various spiritual forces. These unseen powers are part of the world we see and are the ultimate cause of all that happens, especially of unusual and disturbing events. There is no clear dividing line between the physical and the spiritual, between animate and inanimate, between the living and the dead.

All objects are believed to have some degree of life force. Plants have more than rocks and man is near the top of the hierarchy. He is surpassed only by the unseen beings of the spirit world of which there are various kinds.

The ancestors are believed to be in contact with the living and need to be appeased by sacrifices. One may be kept from sleeping by someone who comes to you in his spirit and disturbs you or tries to kill you over a period of time. The power to move about in one's spirit or in the form of an animal is referred to as *magic*, *witchcraft* or *sorcery*, depending on the circumstances. *Gods* are believed to live all over the land and may bring misfortune if not appeased properly. Sorcerers and witches deal with these gods to acquire special powers or riches, often in exchange for the souls of people. It is further believed that many objects have mystical powers so that they can be used to control or manipulate events. Some can be used for *divination* to diagnose a problem or to look into the future. Others are used to make *fetishes* which give the owners special powers or knowledge. Others are made into *charms* to protect the owners from natural disasters or from harm that people or spirits may do to them.

The *ground*, for instance, is often believed to have many mystical powers which it can exert over people, especially over those who are part of a given piece of ancestral land. The ground is used to bless or to ensure good luck. It is called upon as the witness to a vow or promise. It will "catch" or punish the offender and bring peace and prosperity to those who live in accordance with the rules of the ground. These rules were established by the ancestors living on that land and are kept effective by the rituals of family and land priests.

1.2 God, Man and the World

Most, if not all African cultures, also recognize the existence of one *Supreme God*. He is often referred to as God, the Creator, who made man and the world he lives in, including the spiritual powers. But the Creator is believed to be remote from man. He is not readily available to help man. Man rather has to help himself using the means God has put into this world. God is not to be disturbed with the everyday problems of life. Through appropriate ritual and sacrifices man can relate to the spirits in his environment to appease them or to manipulate them. He uses the mystical powers God has given to certain objects to protect himself or to advance his status, riches or knowledge. No matter how powerful certain magic, sorcery or spirits may be, it is believed that "medicines" will always be stronger to overcome these powers. It is just a question of finding the right specialist with the right medicine.

See Figure 1 on page 11: God, Man and the World

1.3 The Extent of the Animistic Worldview

This worldview, which recognizes a multitude of spirit beings and ascribes mystical powers to objects, extends to every sphere of the African's life. It determines his relationships within the family, his relationship to the land on which he lives, and his relationship to the tribe to which he belongs. When looking carefully at how society functions in these **spheres of life (lineage, land, tribe)** it becomes clear that in each one **a spiritual power** is in ultimate control (**ancestor spirits, gods of land and tribe**). This unseen power is the ultimate originator and guardian of the traditions (taboos, rituals and other laws) that govern this sphere of life. It will bring bad luck (sickness, accidents, social strife, natural disasters etc.) to those who ignore or transgress these traditions. But it may also do so out of sheer malevolence or because it has been manipulated to do so by a sorcerer. The visible authority figure in each sphere (**lineage head, landlord, chief**) is actually **a priest or mediator** to that unseen power. He tries to keep the unseen power appeased by rituals and sacrifices and mediates for people who have incurred its wrath. He also invokes the unseen power to bring bad luck to those who transgress the traditions or do not submit to his will in other ways. By enforcing compliance with the traditions he is supposed to uphold the **central value** of his sphere such as, **unity, ritual purity, and peace** *(see Figures 1-5)*.

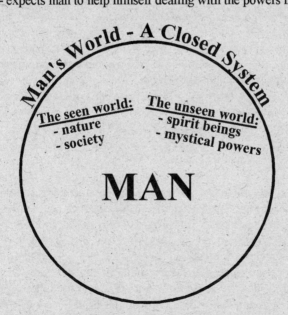

GOD - Creator of good and evil
- remote from man in another world
- placed man into his own world of seen and unseen powers
- expects man to help himself dealing with the powers in his world

Man's World - A Closed System

The seen world:
- nature
- society

The unseen world:
- spirit beings
- mystical powers

MAN

Figure 1: God, Man and the World

1.3.1. The family, ancestors and unity

In relation to the family, most of us are expected to relate, not only to the living members of our families, but also to certain deceased ones, the ancestors. Every one of us is born into a family which is larger than one individual household of a man, his wife and their children. By birth we all become members of a larger group which we shall call the extended family or lineage. This group consists of relatives that are all descended from one common ancestor. We have a strong sense of belonging to this extended family rather than just to an individual household. This is clearly shown in our languages which usually do not distinguish between brothers of the same parents and brothers of the extended family. We refer to them all by the same word. In the same way, we call any older person in our extended family father or mother. When asked about our origin we usually refer to ourselves as "a child of a certain compound" rather than as a child of our actual parents.

These things show that the extended family is very dear to us. It is the social unit to which we belong, which controls us and from which we derive our status in society. Even though I, as an individual, may not be a very important person, I can say that I am a child of this compound which means that the status of my whole extended family reflects on me. The extended family or lineage thus very effectively provides the basic human need of belonging and status.

But the extended family is more than a unit consisting of relatives that are presently living. The family today is what our forefathers made it. It is part of our worldview that at least some of these ancestors are still in contact with the living members of the family that they established. In fact, the ancestors are considered to play a more important role in the affairs of the family than the presently living members. While the living are concerned with life here on earth with all its struggles and temptations, the ancestors, who are free from the struggles of physical life, are concerned with keeping the family on track. This means keeping the family within the traditions of the culture and within any stipulations and rules that they laid down for their families while they were still alive. This sense of control by the ancestors over the living is so strong that some people, who are now being disregarded by their families, sometimes remind them that the time will come when none of them will dare to disregard them.

The living members of the extended family have a direct link to the ancestors through one of their members who functions as the family priest. This person is, in some cultures, called a compound head. He is the leader of the extended family. He derives his power from the fact that he has been chosen as the successor of the deceased compound head and is in direct contact with him and other important ancestors of the family. His power over the family members does not come from any wealth he may possess. Many of his subjects may be wealthier than he, yet they submit to his rulings in family matters.

The greatest moral value that the head of the family tries to uphold within the family is UNITY. Within society each extended family is in opposition to other ones. Dealings between families are regulated by the influence a given family has within society. The larger a family, the greater its chance to make its influence felt. But if the family members are not united the group is weakened. The head of the family will, therefore, always strive for two things: (1) to increase the number of his family, and (2) to have his family united. This unity is often referred to as being of "one mouth." To accomplish this he relies directly on the ancestors.

For example, I might disassociate myself from my family and not fulfill my obligations that are expected of me as a member. Maybe I will stay away from the family without contacting them regularly, or I may refuse to make contributions to family projects such as celebrations or building projects. Another serious offense is to marry off my children without relying on the family head to arrange for the marital contract between our family and the family into which my child marries. All such behavior is commonly referred to as "running away from the family." When a compound head becomes aware of such offenses he will be very concerned to put an end to it. If he does not, other members of the family may imitate my behavior and the family will "scatter."

In order to bring me to my senses, the family head might solicit the help of the ancestors over this, their straying child. He will make a sacrifice, saying something like this to the ancestors, "See our child out there. He has escaped from the family. Bring him back."

He is expecting the ancestors to bring me back by causing some misfortune in my life. For instance, one of my children might get sick. Immediately my thoughts, or those of my wife, will be, "Who is making our child sick? Is it our ancestors, because of my offense against the family, or is it someone else who does not want me to prosper?" To find out I revert to divination. If I do not do this, my family, my wife's family, or my friends will. If it is found out that the ancestors brought this sickness I will have to go to my family head to clear this matter up so that my child will get well. He alone can mediate between me and the ancestors.

One way of mediation is through a sacrifice that the family head performs for me. At that time he asks the ancestors to no longer punish my child but to care for it. However, he will only make this sacrifice if I accept my transgression against the family and make my confession to him and the family council. In this way both the living and the dead members of my family will be satisfied. The UNITY of the family will have been restored, which was the primary concern of the ancestors and the family council. My child will become well, which was my primary concern and that of my wife.

At other times the ancestors may send misfortune on the whole family because of the offense of one of the members. Often these offenses have to do with omission of rituals such as death celebrations and sacrifices, disregard for the final will of the deceased, or a transgression of the intricate rules which govern intermarriage between families. Whatever the problem may be, tremendous pressure is put on the key figure involved to have this problem solved by the appropriate traditional rituals so that the well-being and the unity of the family may be secured.

The compulsion to keep the family unified at any cost makes it difficult to deal with the tensions that naturally arise between members of the family. If a member holds a grudge against another one, he will often look for secret ways to get back at him so that he cannot be accused of destroying the unity of the family. This is one of the reasons why members of an extended family often suspect other members of using witchcraft or magic against them. To protect themselves they may acquire special charms. If that does not help they may flee the family compound leaving their properties behind.

See Figure 2 on page 16: The Lineage - basis of belonging and status

1.3.2 The land, gods and purity

In relation to the land on which they depend for a living, most Africans find themselves tied to some system of nature gods. Land is not usually individually owned but is under the trusteeship of landlords. They parcel the land out to extended families and to individuals for use. Beyond that, their role is that of a land priest. They have to keep the land ceremonially clean so that it will produce crops and be free of gods that might disturb the families who live on that land. The land can become unclean when people transgress against taboo days on which no farm work is to be done, when quarrels break out between extended families, when people fight over parcels of land, when great immoral acts are committed such as incest, when taboo plants and animals are accidentally destroyed, etc. When these things happen the land priest is called upon to perform the rituals necessary to cleanse the land so that the gods who live on this land will not bring disaster on the people.

Another source of trouble are roaming gods. Even though most gods seem to have definitely settled in certain places, there are others that are still roaming around, looking for places to reside. From time to time someone may perceive that a new god has come to an area or to a compound. When this happens, people will be concerned to find out whether the god is a "good" one or a "bad" one. If, by divination, it is found out that the god is bad, they will look to the land priest to perform rituals that will chase this god out of the country. If he is a good one, he will be welcomed and added to the list of gods that need to be appeased in order to keep the land fruitful and in peace.

See Figure 3 on page 17: The Land - basis of subsistence and survival

1.3.3 Man, gods and mystical powers

In many tribes the gods are also considered to be a possible source of wealth and power to individuals. They have powers to make your fields produce more than normal, to give you success in business, to make you succeed in your studies, to show you the herbs that cure certain diseases, etc. Sometimes the gods single out certain individuals to give them certain powers. This frequently happens to children. At birth some children are discerned to have a personal god. In some regions this is especially true of twins. Other children may be visited by a god later. This is often referred to as "a god having stolen the child." When this happens, the child will act strangely, often as if in a trance. In all these instances, special rituals will need to be performed, so that the god of this child will know that he has been recognized and so will not make the child sick. This practice is often called "fixing the child."

The riches that the gods possess are a great attraction for those who have magic. Such people have the power to leave their bodies behind and move about in their spirits. When they do this, they see all the other spirit beings that people without magic do not see. They also see the riches some of these gods have and may become desirous of acquiring some of them. To do that they have to negotiate on a price for a given power. Usually the gods will demand to be paid in human lives. That is, the sorcerer has to turn over to the gods lives of people who are under his control, such as his children or members of the extended family. This is often referred to as "selling people to the devil." If the god is a "bad" one, he will kill those turned over to him. A "good" god may only make the ones sold to him sick in order to show that they are in his power and that they can be redeemed by the right ritual. If this is not done, the people concerned usually die as well.

1.3.4 The tribe, gods and peace

In relation to the tribe as a whole, there are often certain gods believed to live in the land that can only be appeased by the chief of the tribe or his priests. Some ethnic groups have developed elaborate rituals and offerings to these gods to ensure such things as rain falling in the right season, internal and external peace, and general prosperity. When disaster strikes a tribe everybody will immediately suspect that some of the traditions of the country have been neglected. If the rains are not coming at the proper time it may be due to the fact that no offerings have been made on the graves of former chiefs. When many of the elite

15

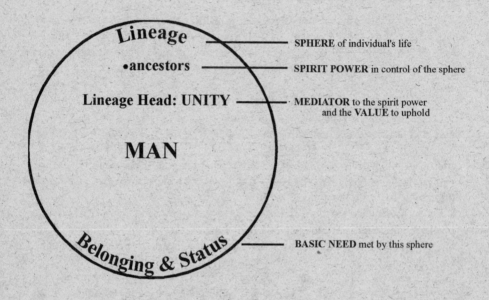

Figure 2: The Lineage – basis of belonging and status

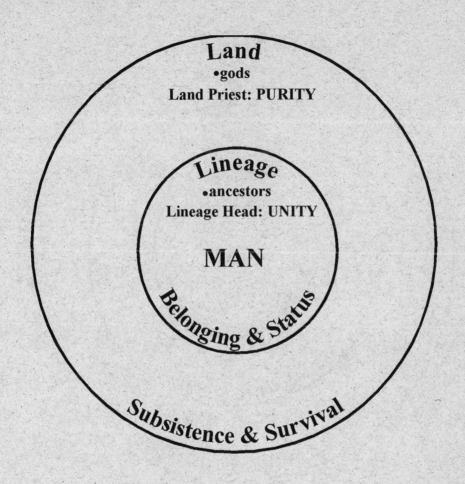

Figure 3: The Land – basis of subsistence and survival

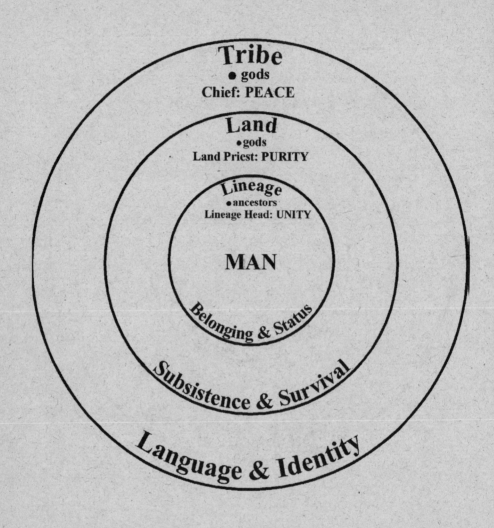

Figure 4: The Tribe – one's identity in the world

18

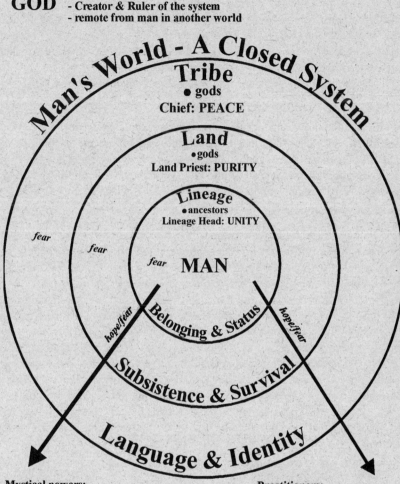

GOD - Creator & Ruler of the system
- remote from man in another world

Man's World - A Closed System

Tribe
● gods
Chief: PEACE

Land
● gods
Land Priest: PURITY

Lineage
● ancestors
Lineage Head: UNITY

MAN

fear *fear* *fear*

hope/fear *hope/fear*

Belonging & Status

Subsistence & Survival

Language & Identity

Mystical powers:
● personal magic
● powers from gods
● witchcraft
● fetishes
● charms

Practitioners:
● diviners (diagnosis)
● priests (appeasement)
● sorcerers (revenge)
● witch doctors (protection)
● fetish societies (status)
● healers (healing)

Figure 5: Cycle of Bondage in ATR to the System

of one language group were experiencing a lot of deaths, illnesses and other misfortunes, they sent a letter to the chief back in their home land, asking him to perform certain rituals in order to avert such disasters. Keeping up the "traditions" is thus important, not only to village dwellers, but also to those members of the tribe who are more educated and hold important positions outside of their actual homelands.

See Figure 4 on page 18: The Tribe - one's identity in the world

1.4 The Effects of the Animistic Worldview

In summary, the animistic worldview which underlies most African cultures usually sees man surrounded by the following spirits: ancestor spirits, the spirits of sorcerers, nature gods, and various mystical powers. These spiritual forces pervade and dominate all of life. This worldview has the following effects on those who adhere to it and in varying degree on those who are influenced by it.

a. It produces fear

People's relationship to these spirits is above all determined by FEAR. Any one of these spirits may bring misfortune into the life of the individual, the family, or the tribe as a whole. Ancestors often bring sickness. Witches and sorcerers are after the lives of others, either out of revenge, jealousy, or in order to acquire riches from the gods. Even gods who are believed to favor an individual will cause that person to become crazy or to die if they are not properly recognized. The individual who has magic seeks to manipulate the spirit forces for his own advancement and enrichment, but he, too, lives in fear. He knows that dealing with the spirit world is dangerous because every advantage one might gain also has its price. Nothing is for free. He also fears others magicians who are constantly testing him with their own powers, hoping to destroy him in order to enrich themselves. Within the circle of the extended family this worldview sows suspicion and fear because it is in this circle that witchcraft is most often practiced.

b. It produces bondage

For hope to deal with problems perceived to originate from the spirit world one turns inward to the system of mystical powers and to practitioners who can harness them and manipulate spirit beings. One looks to divination to diagnose the problem and manipulate the future; to sacrifices and offerings to appease capricious ancestors and gods; and to charms and fetishes for protection against nature, human magic and spirits. At the same time one fears each of these powers and practitioners because dealing with them binds one to powers that are unpredictable and often outright malevolent, so that one can never be sure of the long-term consequences. The system does not provide access to flee to God for help. In fact, in this worldview God, too, is not truly good and trustworthy since he is seen as the one who created this system and ordained it to work as it does. Thus the ATR worldview systems binds its adherents in a vicious cycle of bondage back to the system.

c. It offers only superficial solutions to felt needs

The system tries to respond to genuine felt needs in the life of the tribe such as family solidarity, fertility of the land, and general prosperity of the tribe. The system therefore upholds certain values such as UNITY of the family, RITUAL PURITY of the land, and PEACE at the level of the tribe. These values are noble ones. However, all the animistic worldview has to offer is a system of fear that produces, at best, only superficial unity, purity and peace. For instance, in Nso' families outward unity is such a high value that differences are buried below the surface resulting in long-standing grudges and at times the use of magical powers to take secret revenge. Grudges get carried on beyond the grave and some people count on getting even from the other side of the grave when, as ancestor spirits, they have greater powers at their disposal. This is expressed in a nut shell by the Nso' proverb which says, "The worst quarrel you could have is one with an ancestor."

See Figure 5 on page 19: Cycle of Bondage in ATR to the System

2.0 Christianity and the African Worldview

2.1 The Appeal of Christianity to Traditional Africans

Christianity has experienced phenomenal growth in Africa among the adherents of traditional African religion since its first introduction by the early missionaries. Christianity continues to grow in numbers and popularity to the extent that most Africans coming from a animistic background want to be considered Christians today. To be considered a pagan is an insult.

This appeal of Christianity to the traditional African is basically due to the fact that the gospel message provides the answer to a big void that ATR left in the hearts of its adherents, namely the relationship of man to the Supreme God. ATR recognizes the existence of the Supreme God, but man cannot reach out to him. He is condemned to deal with the spirits that rule the world he lives in. There are mediators to the various spiritual powers: the family head to the ancestors; the landlord to the gods of the land; the king and his priests to the gods of the country; and a variety of specialists mediate and facilitate access by the common man to the mystical powers of charms, fetishes and divination. But in ATR there is no mediator to the Supreme God; there is no hope of life with God in paradise. Though, in various ethnic groups, traditions exist that talk of a contact with God in the past and a hope of paradise, but these have been irretrievably lost to man. Thus, when the message of the gospel came to Africa proclaiming Christ as the mediator to God and the way to paradise, it provided the answer to a deep felt need within the heart of the traditional African.

There are many other valuable points of contact between ATR and the message of the Bible that have facilitated the advance of Christianity. Some of these are a consciousness of and, in some groups, a preoccupation with guilt, the need for cleansing, and the centrality of the blood sacrifice for cleansing and release from judgment. These and many other aspects of ATR are also important elements of the Biblical message of redemption. In ATR they are for the most part degenerated deviations from the biblical truths, but they, nevertheless, represent powerful analogies that have contributed to the appeal of Christianity to the traditional African.

The Christian counselor needs to be aware of these dynamics within ATR both for their potential for communicating the biblical message, as well as for the danger they pose of creating a non-biblical Christianity if these faulty and degenerate concepts of ATR are not corrected in the Church through teaching and practices that are biblically sound and culturally effective.

2.2 The Dilemma of the African Christian

In this section we will look at some issues arising out of the African worldview and at the way the church has addressed these issues that have a negative influence on the growth and development of the Christian and the African church as a whole.

2.2.1 The dilemma of a non-African gospel

The African Christian often finds it difficult to identify with the Scriptural view of the spirit world. It does not seem to match the worldview that he absorbed from earliest childhood. Most African Christians do not have access to a translation of the Scriptures in their own languages, so they read in a second language or, for the most part, learn about it through interpreters. This not only limits access by the believers to the Scriptures which is the only sure foundation for a biblical faith, but it virtually makes it impossible for the truth of the Bible to become alive in the cultures of these people. Many biblical truths will not speak to the listener as relevant to his situation because they do not come across in the terms of his daily cultural experiences.

For instance, the Bible has much to say about the spirit world, the topic so important to the African worldview. However, since each ethnic group usually recognizes a multitude of spirits, most interpreters and pastors will use a loan word to translate the Scripture term "demon," or they may give a literal translation of the term "evil spirit." In most African languages this comes across as "bad breath." Whichever term they use, it is not usually a culturally familiar one. This gives the listener the impression that the spirits mentioned in the Bible are unique to the Jewish culture. In other words, what the Bible has to say about spirits applies to Jewish "country fashion" but not to their own.

2.2.2 The inconsistency between teaching and practice

Pastors and Christian teachers have often strengthened this impression unknowingly. Believers often hear them say that their traditional religion and its practices are things of the past and that the Bible wants them to forsake such foolish practices. But Africans know that their own spirits are very powerful and fearsome, so the Bible must be talking about a different "country fashion." Furthermore, the believers know very well that the pastor, who denies the power of the traditional religion from the pulpit, is in reality very much afraid of the spirit forces active in their culture. This type of preaching has fostered the impression among Christians that their faith has very little to do with their everyday living. One old mother summed this up by telling her preacher son, "Christianity is believing, not living."

2.2.3 Prohibitions without biblical solutions

Every animistic practice is geared to meet a certain human need. The Christian who has grown up with an animistic worldview "sees spirits everywhere." To tell him that he should not put his trust in charms for protection against spirits does not help, especially if he cannot sleep at night because the spirit of a witch disturbs him. When the child of a Christian displays symptoms which indicate that a god has stolen the spirit of the child, the Christian is not helped by just telling him not to consult a sorcerer. He is certain that his child will die if its spirit is not released by the gods. But very few pastors go beyond the prohibition to deal with the problems at hand. So the Christian is led to believe that the gospel has no answer to his need. He, therefore, has to help himself through traditional means that have previously proven effective.

All this has spawned the popular impression among Christians that our hope in Christ is something for the future only. We believe now in Christ so that we will go into the kingdom of heaven after this earthly life. Salvation is from hell to come, and eternal life starts only after death. The Christian who has gained this impression of his faith reverts easily to animistic practices when disaster of one kind or another strikes because he sees no help offered by Christianity.

2.2.4 The practice of rationalizing help from any source

To justify this life of duplicity some argue that many of the rituals, charms and even gods of their own culture are not really evil. They are good as long as they can help us. In a discussion of the topic of healing practices, a pastor of many years said that the person who is sick should be free to look to any source for help without asking himself what powers a given healer relies on to heal him. He then related from his own experience how he had been healed from a prolonged sickness by a healer who used his magic to remove objects from his body that a sorcerer had put into it. He went on to say that all healing powers in the end come from God, whether they are given to men, to spirits or to objects, and that God expects us to use what he has provided. He concluded that something which can heal cannot be evil.

2.2.5 Confusion about cultural versus biblical good

Within the various cultures many powers and practices are referred to as "good." Some Christians think that everything that is labeled good in their culture must be one of the "good and perfect gifts" coming from God. There is good magic; there are good gods; and there are good charms. One pastor was wondering whether the "good" gods their culture speaks about are not the angels the Scriptures talk about. Pastors have made little effort to teach Christians how to decide what is good in the Scriptural sense and what is not. Many, rather, condemn all of the "country fashion" as evil and contrary to the Scriptures. This does more harm than good, because there are many aspects of a given culture which fulfill good and God-given functions. The social structure of a culture, for instance, fulfills the God-intended purpose that on earth every person should be responsible to someone. In summary, the Christians usually hear only two points of view from their leaders. There are those who say everything that can help man in some way must be good. Then there are others who say that everything of the traditional culture is pagan worship, and therefore wrong.

2.2.6 The dilemma of social pressure

The Christian is not only faced with a confusing and inconsistent approach by the church towards the traditions of his culture, but he is also under great social pressure from within his culture to comply with many of the practices of animism. He may be under pressure by his wife or her relatives to have a sacrifice performed for the health of their child. His own family will put him under pressure to perform all the rituals in connection with his parents' death, because the dead can bring ill luck on the whole family. An agreement between two may not be valid unless certain rituals are performed. Also if one abstains from certain rituals and ceremonies, one loses esteem in the family and in society as a whole. Beyond that, the individual's loss of esteem is always a loss for the whole family, and so family pressure is again brought to bear on the individual to live in a traditional way.

2.2.7 The temptation of proven traditional methods

Participating in animistic rituals and practices presents a great temptation to the Christian. Through them he may avoid certain misfortunes or advance his influence. Belonging to a secret society may advance your status in your clan as well as in the tribe. The most popular people in a "Christianized" tribe are often those who go to church and participate in everything else without discriminating between good traditions and pagan practices.

2.2.8 Summary

In summary, the Christian's dilemma in relating to the spirit world as seen by his culture is this: the Bible does not seem to say anything about spirits known to his culture; the teachings of the church on the topic are confusing and impractical (some ridicule the traditional religion yet secretly they fear it, others condemn the whole traditional culture as pagan without recognizing the good parts in it, others teach that whatever is useful must also be good, and many do not teach anything but let people do what they think is best); often the church does not offer help with the problems that traditional practices address; the Christian knows the powers of the spirit world and fears them, but he has not seen the power of God demonstrated with regards to his cultural problems; the individual is under a great social pressure to comply with the traditions; and it is very tempting to rely on proven traditional ways for problem solving and self advancement.

2.3 The Dilemma of the African Church

2.3.1 The dilemma of syncretism

In many areas where the gospel has been proclaimed for many decades, the church today is faced with the problem of syncretism. By this we mean that Christians try to combine their faith with some aspects of the animistic religion. Some people do that consciously, especially certain intellectuals, who argue that all the religious practices of their forefathers were part of God's revelation to man and that Christianity has only added certain aspects to their traditional way of worship. Most people, however, slip into syncretism unconsciously. They worship God as Christians and do not intend to worship other deities or spirits. However, they find themselves confronted in everyday life with many problems and fears for which the "traditions of home" offer certain solutions through divination, sacrifices and charms, while the Christian leaders usually do not address these problems. Consequently, many turn to these pagan practices for help and start to live double lives. They look to their Christian faith for final salvation but look to pagan practices for present help. They do not realize that by doing this they are putting themselves into the clutches of Satan, whose plan is to darken their minds so they will not know God (2 Corinthians 4:4). The greatest tragedy is that most Christian leaders do not seem to recognize how Satan is active in this way amongst the Christians. They need to awaken to this and recognize that Satan's purpose is always "to kill and to destroy the sheep" (John 10:10).

2.3.2 The practice of leaving social leadership to pagans

Another tragic outcome is that in many Christianized areas very few traditional rulers are practicing Christians. This applies to tribal chiefs, clan heads, and family heads. Whenever one of these is chosen, the very people who confess to be Christians will usually look for a candidate who is able to perform all the pagan rituals connected with this position. They do this mostly out of fear, because they are afraid that disaster will strike if these traditions are not upheld. The result is that, although the majority of the people may claim to be Christians and want to live the Christian life, they live in social structures that are controlled by Satanic forces. Christians need to be liberated from their fear of the spirit world so that they will dare to become true Christian leaders in their society or support Christian candidates for leadership. In this way whole extended families will be wrenched from the direct influence of Satan and his spirits and brought under the influence of Christ.

2.3.3 The lack of appeal of Christianity to men

The fact that Christians have largely delegated leadership in society to practicing pagans, or to compromising Christians, has doubtless contributed to the fact that in many areas the men do not take the Christian faith seriously. Our churches are filled with women, for which we praise God, but where are the men? In African societies leadership is very much the function of the men. This includes leadership in the individual household. Leadership largely means finding solutions to the problems of here and now. The traditional culture has worked out mechanisms for dealing with these problems in one way or another. The methods usually combine good social principles with pagan rituals that spring from the animistic worldview. Christianity for the most part has prohibited its adherents from making use of these methods of problem solving, but has not offered new ways of dealing with the problems at hand. No wonder that the men, who are the leaders in society, often reject the Christian faith as impractical.

2.3.4 The lack of fathers as spiritual leaders

A direct result of this has been that very few households of our church members function as Christian families in which the father is the spiritual leader. The role of the Christian father is to represent God to the family, so that by observing him they may learn in some measure what God is like - that he is love but is also holy and righteous. The Christian life is one of worship. This means having access to God and letting him work in our lives so that he can change our hearts, comfort us and strengthen us in life's problems. Animism is not a way of worship. It does not provide a way to God. It does not seek to change the heart of man through the power of God. It rather seeks to avert disaster by appeasing or manipulating the spirit world. Fathers who are Christians in name only cannot show God to their children because they are not allowing God to work in them. They do not understand the role parents have in character building. Rather than passing on Christian values to their children through personal example, teaching and family worship, they let problems develop fatalistically and then try to deal with these as best they can in traditional ways. To them, character is something a child is born with. Some are born to be good men, others to be thieves. All we can do is try to avert disaster by manipulating the spirit world.

2.3.5 Christianity is seen as modern progress

Because of all these factors the Christian faith has had little impact on the culture of many African peoples. Christianity is looked upon as something in addition to one's traditional culture and religion, rather than the power of God to work within that culture. Christianity is popularly identified with some of the aspects of progress that have come in the wake of missionary efforts. Christians have seen the "light" of progress in education, health, employment, etc. Pagans still live in "the world of darkness" that has not yet been opened up by the "light" of modern civilization. In addition, Christianity offers the hope of an eternal life which animism does not offer. Such a faith can be easily combined with animism. It does not contradict animism but supplements it. Through the "light" of Christianity one reaps the benefits of modern progress. Through the "traditions" one guards oneself from anything that might block this progress. Beyond that, the "Christian" may gain an eternal future. This conception of Christianity is very widespread among Christians and pagans alike. It is one of the reasons why Christianity is so attractive to the peoples of unevangelized regions. They often request Christian workers to come to their region to bring them the "light." Nobody wants to live in "darkness" any more.

2.3.6 The dilemma of numbers versus discipling

This type of popularity presents the church with a tremendous opportunity but also with a tremendous challenge. The challenge is to withstand the temptation of easy evangelism that boasts only in numbers and leaves the people chained in fear. In each culture the strongholds of Satan need to be identified and destroyed in the life of the Christian through the power of the Spirit of God. Only then will the believer know the reality of the Christian faith and know that the same power of God which liberated him from the power of Satan will also keep him until the day Christ returns. The light of the gospel is not modern progress but the power of God in this life to defeat the power of Satan. Our commission today is still the same which Christ gave to Paul in Acts 25:17-18, "I am sending you to them to open their eyes and turn them from darkness to light, and from the power of Satan to God, so that they may receive forgiveness of sins and a place among those who are sanctified by faith in me."

2.3.7 Summary

In summary, Satan has his strongholds in every culture. In many African cultures Satan's greatest stronghold on people is through the animistic worldview which condemns man in this life to deal with the spirits rather than directly with God. If the Christian message only presents hope for a future salvation it is not the true message, nor does it create true children of God. The true message is first and foremost one of liberation. The true child of God is one who has turned from the power of Satan and experiences now in this life the power of God. We, as Christian workers, need to know how Satan is working within our cultures, and in our churches, in order to tear down these strongholds through the power of the Spirit of God so that God will be seen among his people. We dare not condemn any culture as a whole as ungodly, because every culture is the expression of the God-ordained law that man live under authority to someone (Romans 13:1,2) and the expression of the God-given desire by man to seek after God (Acts 17:26,27). What we need to know is what aspects of our cultures Satan is exploiting and how we can develop biblical approaches for these situations to meet the needs of the believers and to destroy the strongholds of Satan in their lives.

To know Satan's strongholds we need to interpret our cultures in light of what Scripture has revealed about the nature and work of Satan and his demons. In section 3 some of the basic biblical facts about spiritual realities are sketched before proceeding, in section 4, to an interpretation of ATR in light of these facts.

3.0 The Biblical View of Spiritual Realities

As we have seen, the spirit world is central to African traditional religion and to the worldview that has come from there. As biblical Christians we believe that the Bible is God's revelation to man which contains all the essentials of what we need to know with regards to God, his creation and our relationship to Him and the world. Thus, in order to discern truth here on earth we need to constantly evaluate all areas of human knowledge, experience and practice in light of the truths revealed in the Bible and the principles established there. This is especially true when it comes to the realm of the unseen powers in this world. We therefore need to first establish what the Bible has revealed about the spirit world before we can proceed to interpret ATR and our African cultures in view of this.

3.1 The Authority of the Bible to Judge Cultures

The Scriptures were written over a period of 2,000 years beginning about 4,000 years ago. Much of it was addressed to the people of the Jewish culture. Some people, therefore, argue that what the Bible says about spiritual powers and their manifestations is peculiar to the Jewish culture and does not necessarily apply to their cultures. However, we have to recognize that God chose the Jews as a channel through which He would eventually make himself known to all nations (Genesis 12:3).

Before God chose Abraham, the Jewish culture did not exist. God made the descendants of Abraham into a nation so that they would a holy people, different from all the other nations (Lev. 19:2). He revealed himself to them over a long period of time, shaping their culture and worldview so that it would reflect his eternal truth and principles. All along God's aim was that His Son should come as a Jew to show within that culture, as a message to all the world, what He, the Father, is really like (John 1:18). We can, therefore, look to the Bible as the authoritative guide which gives us, within its record of God revealing himself to man within his culture, the basic facts that are needed to discern, in any culture, what is of God and what is not.

This does not mean that the spirit world manifests itself in every culture the way it did in the Jewish culture. Over the whole period of revelation God addressed the different manifestations of evil powers in other nations and warned his people about them. In the days of the early Christian church, God was calling his people out of many different cultures with different religious backgrounds and different manifestations of evil in each culture. Some worshipped angels, others practiced immorality as part of their cults, others worshipped the king, and many Jews believed in rituals such as circumcision rather than God. The epistles deal with many of these problems. They show us how to interpret culture in view of God's revelation about Himself and the spirit world, and how to test the spirits.

3.2 Spiritual Realities as Revealed in the Bible

a. The Supreme God

First of all, the Bible reveals clearly the existence of God as Creator and Supreme Ruler of the universe. He is infinite in time and power, as well as in holiness and goodness (Rev.4:8-11). He is sovereign over all things, including evil, and makes everything ultimately serve his good purposes (Ps.2:4-6; Eph.4: 8-11). There is only one God, but he exists in three persons, the Father, the Son, and the Holy Spirit. In relation to man, God the Father is the creator and sustainer of life, the provider of man's needs and the source of his redemption. As God the

Son, he reveals himself to man and accomplishes his redemption. As God the Holy Spirit, he renews fallen man and empowers him for life and service.

b. The angels

The Bible also tells us that God created a host of angels who are his ministering spirits. Since they are spirits they are not bound to the physical universe the way human beings are. In the Scriptures they are described as winds and flames of fire which emphasizes the fact that they are powerful, invisible, and freely move through the universe (Hebrews 1:7). God created the angels in a perfect state to be his servants and to worship him (Hebrews 1:6).They have various functions in God's kingdom. They surround God's throne to worship and praise him (Isa.6:1-7; Rev.5:11,12); they minister to believers (Heb.1:14; Acts 12:6-11; Ps.91:11-12); they execute judgment for God (Gen.19; Acts 12:3; Rev.15:1); they fight demons for control of nations (Dan 10:13,20;12:1); they have some control over natural forces (Rev.7:1); they are involved in ushering in the end of the age (Mt.13:41-2).

c. The fallen angels: Satan and his demons

However, some of the angels rebelled against God under the leadership of Lucifer, the prince of the angels, who wanted to make himself equal to God (Isaiah 14:12-15 and Luke 10:18). We are told that God did not spare these angels who sinned, because he is holy and his character can have no part in evil (2 Peter 2:4). We know that Satan and those angels who rebelled with him were cast out of heaven (Revelation 12:7-11), and that God prepared hell as a place of judgment for Satan and his angels (Matthew 25:41). We are told in 2 Peter 2:4 that some of the angels are chained up awaiting their judgment but others, under the leadership of Satan, are free to roam the earth until their final day of judgment comes. In Ephesians 2:1,2 Satan is called the ruler of the Kingdom of the air. This means Satan is the ruler of spirits which can freely move through the air. The Scripture calls these spirits demons, evil spirits or unclean spirits. Satan, as their king, is also called Beelzebub (Matthew 12:24). The demons at his control are very powerful. The Scriptures refer to them in Ephesians 6:12 as "rulers and authorities," and as "spiritual forces of evil." It warns us that we cannot fight the demons with human strength but only with the armour of God (Ephesians 6: 13-18).

3.3 The Work of Satan and his Demons

a. Satan's target is man

When Satan was cast out of heaven with his demons he was allowed to be active on earth. From the first pages in the Bible it is shown that Satan's purposes have always been to destroy the work of God in every way possible. When God created man, Satan immediately aimed at separating man from God and bringing man under his control. He appealed to man's desire to be independent from God, to decide for himself what is good and what is evil. Man fell, not realizing that he would become dependent on Satan. Being separated from God, man lost his innocence and became subject to a fallen nature, which tends toward evil, and is well disposed toward suggestions by Satan.

b. Satan's aim is ruling the world

Not only did man become a sinful being, but with him all creation fell, because God had put it under man's control. This world became imperfect, full of troubles, hardships and disasters. Everything became subject to death (Romans 8:20). Satan seemed to have won the battle for this world by getting man, the head of the creation, on his side. He set up his kingdom on earth and in the sky to control this world through demons. His aim is to keep man in transgressions and sins and thereby dead to God (Ephesians 2:1-2).

c. Satan failed in preventing the Kingdom of God on earth

But God in his mercy provided for the salvation of man in Jesus Christ. He revealed this even to Adam and Eve. He told the snake that an offspring of Eve would eventually crush him (Genesis 3:15).By faith in God's promise, Adam and Eve were able to become members of the kingdom of God that Christ would bring. However, Satan was not going to give up without a fight. He was determined to prevent the coming of Christ, so that the Kingdom he would bring would never become a reality. Throughout history Satan worked hard to destroy the nation of Israel through which the Saviour would come. When he did not succeed in this, he tried to have King Herod kill the new-born Jesus, but again he failed. The temptation of Christ was a repetition of the temptation of man in Eden. Satan appealed to the Son of God to become independent, to decide by himself what was good for him rather than trusting God. But Christ withstood the temptation and accepted God's will for him whether that meant hunger in the desert, rejection by man, or even death on the cross. By his complete obedience to God, Christ defeated Satan in his plan to prevent the redemption of man (John 16:11, Colossians 2:15). Now all those who put their trust in Christ have a perfect Saviour from sin and the power of Satan.

d. Satan tries to blind unbelievers to the gospel

Satan knows he is judged and redemption is secured for those who trust in Christ, but he still has not relented. His purpose today is to "blind the minds of the unbelievers so that they cannot see the light of the gospel" (2 Corinthians 4:4).

e. Satan tries to make believers ineffective for God

His aim with the believers is to make them ineffective for God. He opposes their work for God by maneuvering circumstances and events to block their plans (1 Thessalonians 2:18)l; he tries to destroy the unity of believers (2 Corinthians 2:11); he tries to lead them into sin such as immorality (1 Corinthians 7:5;1 Timothy 5:15); he tries to make them doubt God by giving them suffering (2 Corinthians 12:7) and persecution (Revelation 2:10). His ways are myriad and we should not be ignorant of them.

f. Satan controls cultures and societies through demons

Satan does much of his work through demons. His kingdom is well organized to oppose the kingdom of God. Through his demons Satan can be in many places at the same time and control events to a certain degree. We are told in the book of Daniel (10:12,13,20,21) that certain demons are assigned to control rulers of countries. From this we can conclude that the same is happening on all levels of leadership such as tribes, towns, villages, and compounds. In the Church "deceiving spirits" are particularly active by encouraging false teaching (1 Timothy 4:1-3).

g. Demons give mysterious powers but exact a price

We are told by Christ that demons move around in this world without a body, but they prefer to live in a person in order to have a body to live in and to control (Matthew 12:43-45). In some cases the demons give special powers to those they possess like the slave girl in Philippi who had the power to predict the future (Acts 16:16). Others possess superhuman strength like the demoniac who broke chains and iron fetters (Mark 5:4) or the one who overcame the seven sons of Sceva (Acts 19:16). But the most common symptom of demon possession is some kind of suffering that the demons give the possessed person such as madness, self-mutilation (Mark 5:5),convulsions (Mark 9:18), blindness and muteness (Matthew 12:22), and self-destruction (Mark 9:22).

h. Satan promotes false religions

Satan's aim in all his work is to keep man separated from God. One of his main tactics to this end is the promotion of false religions so that man might worship anything but God. His demons are active in these religions to lend them mystical powers in order to deceive the adherents and bind them to the system. The Bible tells us that those who worshipped idols in the Greek culture in reality worshipped demons without knowing it (1. Cor 10:18-20). In different cultures this false worship takes different forms. It may be worship of stars, the earth, animals, angels or ancestor and nature spirits as in traditional Africa. In every case this worship is offered to demons and ultimately to their master, Satan, whom the Bible calls the "god of this age" (2 Cor. 4:4).

To sum up, the aim of Satan and his demons is always to destroy men by keeping them from eternal life offered in Christ alone. Christ called the devil "a murderer from the beginning" (John 8:44). His main method is deceiving people by leading them into false worship. He is the "father of lies" (John 8:44) and he presents himself as an angel of light rather than showing his real nature (2 Corinthians 11:14).

4.0 Interpreting ATR in View of Scripture

Comparing the ATR view of spiritual realities with the one revealed in the Scripture we see certain similarities as well as differences. For example, ATR agrees with Scripture in assuming the existence of a Supreme Being who is the Creator, but it differs with Scripture as to the exact character of God, his role in the universe, and his relationship to man.

We are not concerned here with a detailed comparison of all the different aspects of ATR with biblical revelation. Others have produced such studies (e.g. Gehman 1989). Our concern is rather with the larger categories of truth and error in ATR that have become part of a general worldview common to people with an ATR background. What are some of the traditional beliefs that Africans in general hold about God and the spirit world that overlap with Scripture and can be used as points of contact in the process of Christian communication? Also, what are the crucial misconceptions coming out of ATR that need to change in a person's worldview in order for him to come to a true knowledge of God and the Christian life?

4.1 Elements of Truth in ATR

a. Existence of God

The existence of God as the Supreme Being above all spiritual beings is generally assumed in ATR. God is known as the Creator of the universe. He is also seen as the Sustainer of it though in a more detached way from the biblical view. Generally God is recognized as omnipotent and omnipresent. The weakest area of knowledge about God seems to be in the area of his holiness and goodness..

b. The concept of creation

This concept is differently expressed in the various forms of ATR though creation is always assumed. There is no room in the African worldview for a universe that came about by chance.

33

c. The reality of the spirit world

Knowledge of the spirit world lies at the very heart of ATR. Various spirit beings are recognized. Some are closely tied to the human anatomy; others are separate spiritual beings, but they all affect man greatly. The biblical message about the existence of Satan and demons, as well as angels, hits a very familiar chord in the ATR worldview. However, ATR differs fundamentally from Scripture as to their character, their role in the universe, and their relationship to God and man.

d. Man's spiritual nature

ATR agrees with Scripture that man is essentially a spiritual being. He is not only body but has a spiritual side to him which links him to the supernatural while he is alive and continues to exist when the body dies. In ATR, however, the departed do not leave earth for another distant sphere, be it paradise or hell. They rather stay in close proximity to the living as ancestor spirits who are much involved in the affairs of their living descendants.

e. Estrangement from God

A general concept in ATR is that God is very distant from man, at least as far as his involvement in man's affairs is concerned. This concept overlaps partially with the Scriptural teaching of man's estrangement from God because of sin. In most African cultures it is not exactly known why God is so distant. It is rather unquestioningly accepted as a fact. In some cultures, however, there are traditions of God having been close to man in the distant past but having withdrawn in anger because of some offense committed by man. However, ATR completely lacks the concept of God seeking out fallen man to bridge this gap.

f. The concept of substitutionary death

The practice of offerings and sacrifices to spirit beings is very central to ATR practices. Offerings of food and drink are frequently brought to keep gods and ancestors appeased. But at particular times animal sacrifices are made. The underlying idea of the sacrifice is that the life of an animal is given as a substitute for the life of a person, so that the spirits will be appeased and the person freed from their clutches. Furthermore, the person requesting the sacrifice is usually required to confess before the elders what he has done to make the spirits angry. Even though the sacrifices in ATR are made to spirits and not to God, the very ideas of substitution and confession in ATR make it easy for the traditional African to understand the biblical truth of the substitutionary death of Christ and how to appropriate it personally through confession.

g. Values

As has already been seen in an earlier section, in some African societies the values most highly esteemed in the domains of the extended family, the land and the tribe are UNITY, PURITY and PEACE respectively. These values are also biblical ones though ATR differs from the biblical faith in how to achieve them. ATR relies largely on FEAR of the spirit beings in charge of the various domains of life to enforce its system of values. The biblical faith relies rather on the Holy Spirit who regenerates fallen man and sets him free to serve God out of loyalty and to love his fellow man.

However, the value system of ATR overlaps substantially with that of the Bible; much more so than today's Western value system does. Africans value community, sharing of possessions, character over riches or knowledge, and respect for elders. Many of these values have been largely destroyed in Western culture by the forces of individualism, materialism and extreme insistence on personal rights over against those of the community.

4.2 The Source of Truth and Error in ATR

There are other elements of residual truth in ATR that one could list. However, the important point here is to put this matter of truth in ATR into perspective. As has already been indicated under the various points, each element of truth in ATR is surrounded by serious error so that the system as a whole leads man away from God rather than towards God. ATR cannot be regarded as a belief system that can be redeemed by adding further light from the Scriptures. The elements of truth in ATR are rather points of contact or bridges that facilitate an understanding of the truth as it comes through the Scriptures.

It should be of no surprise that we find elements of truth in ATR, as indeed we do in all religions, because God has not left himself without a witness. He reveals himself to man everywhere in his creation (Psalm 19:1) and by his gracious deeds (Mt. 5:45). Furthermore, God has put the knowledge of his law into man's heart or conscience (Rom 2:15). But man's knowledge of God from these sources depends on man's perception of what he sees in nature and in his heart. Man is a fallen creature and his heart, as well as his senses, are subject to sin and to the deception of Satan. This corrupting influence on the knowledge of God as it comes through natural revelation is the source of all false religions in the world. Thus, in spite of many elements of truths in the various religions, outside of the biblical revelation all men live in ignorance of God (Acts 17:30). They worship the creature rather than the Creator (Rom. 1:25), and are blinded by Satan from seeing the truth (2 Cor 4:4).

Religion is man's effort to reach out to God in accordance with the desire God has put into his heart (Acts 17:27). ATR is one expression of this desire.

Like all other non-biblical religions it is built around some truths yet totally incapable of leading men to God. The call of the Scriptures to people of all religions it to repent and turn to Christ who brings God to them (Acts 17:30,31).Knowing that man in his depraved state could never know him on his own (Rom 3:8-10), God decided to reach out to man in Christ to redeem him and to give him his Spirit so that he may know the Truth and walk in it.

The Christian communicator and counselor need to be aware of the elements of truth in ATR as well as the context of deceptions in which they occur. The elements of truth are valuable points of departure in communication to proceed from the known to the unknown. However, it is just as important, and probably even more important, to understand how a given truth in ATR is used to support a system of false worship. If this is not understood false beliefs and error may continue undetected, even when outward forms of worship change.

4.3 Crucial Misconceptions Underlying ATR

By misconceptions underlying ATR we mean basic concepts in the worldview of the ATR adherent that are wrong from biblical perspective and give the person a false view of reality. The semi-conceptions are deception worked by sin and Satan in the area of truth. Deceptions in truth lead to deceptions in deeds. One misconception typically gives birth to a wide variety of wrong practices. Our concern here is with those misconceptions that are crucial in the sense that they are major strongholds of Satan in the ATR worldview and need to be corrected if a person is ever to truly know God and enjoy the Christian life in its fullness. Too many African Christians are tempted to revert back to traditional practices in times of crisis, because some of these crucial misconceptions have never been corrected in their worldview. They are bound by wrong fears and become easy prey to Satan's traps within their own culture.

a. ATR views the spirit world as one unified system under God

The ATR worldview sees the spirit world as only one hierarchy with God on the top. Gods, divinities, nature and ancestor spirits are all seen as God-ordained powers to rule in certain domains as God delegated these areas to them. They are God's surrogates with whom man deals instead of dealing with God directly. They can be considered mediators to God, though in a removed sense, because they do not take man's affairs to God but rather deal with them on God's behalf.

ATR recognizes that many of these spirits are malevolent and that even those considered "good" are unpredictable. They are all to be feared for the evil they can bring. God sanctions the whole system and presides over it. Both "good" and "evil" powers in the spirit world ultimately come from him. To help man live in this precarious environment, he provided him with rituals and mystical powers within the system to protect himself and to manipulate the spirit world to his advantage. Spirits are seen as being capable of any kind of evil while God is generally considered to be good and the author of all the good things. However, since God is seen as the author of this system of a mixture of good and evil doubt is cast on the character of God by association. The ATR adherent is not sure about the character of God and whether his intentions for man are always for good. God is not fully trustworthy, but then it does not really matter since he is not accessible anyway.

Biblical revelation in contrast to ATR recognizes two opposing spiritual systems in the world, the Kingdom of God and the Kingdom of Satan, also called the Kingdom of Light and the Kingdom of Darkness respectively. Even though God is the Creator of all things, he is not the author of evil. He does not sanction the Kingdom of Darkness, nor does he rely on it to accomplish his purposes in the world.

God is the head of the Kingdom of Light while Satan heads the Kingdom of Darkness. The Kingdom of Darkness opposes the Kingdom of Light and is a counterfeit of it. Thus both kingdoms are organized similarly. The holy angels of God are opposed by the demons of Satan. Both kingdoms are invisible now. Their rule is rather established in the hearts of men which are the focus of the battle between the two kingdoms. For man there is no middle ground. Whether he is aware of it or not, he belongs either to one kingdom or the other. ATR totally lacks this distinction between the two opposing kingdoms, resulting in the following:

- God is not wholly good and cannot be fully trusted;
- Dealing with spirits and mystical powers is legitimized, binding man to the Kingdom of Darkness;
- Idolatry in the form of spirit and ancestor worship is encouraged.

Scripture clearly forbids dealings with spirits and mystical powers because Satan, the "god of this age", is active behind these powers through his demons. Each entanglement with the spirit world opens a door for demon attachment and ties man more and more to the Kingdom of Darkness so that he will not see the light of the Gospel (2 Cor. 4:4). In Deuteronomy 18:9-13 Israel is clearly forbidden all contact with the spirit world, including sacrifices to other gods, divination, sorcery, interpretation of omens, witchcraft, casting of spells, consulting of mediums and consulting of the dead (see also Lev. 19:26-31; Isa. 8:18-20). In the Old Testament the punishment for wizards, mediums, and sorcerers was death (Ex. 22:18; Lev. 20:27). In the New Testament sorcery is listed as one of the works of the flesh (Gal 5:20) and sorcerers are excluded from the heavenly Jerusalem (Rev. 21:8; 22:15).

ATR legitimizes all these forbidden practices and encourages them by claiming that they are all part of the God-ordained system. This is a clever lie of Satan and a major stronghold in the ATR worldview which needs to be drastically adjusted in light of Scripture. Only Scripture gives the true picture of the spiritual realities in the world. The following chart attempts to contrast the ATR view of spiritual realities in the world with the biblical one. In the middle column the ATR view is outlined with its mixture of truth and error. To the left and right of the ATR column parallel elements of the Kingdom of God and that of Satan are listed to allow for comparison and interpretation of the ATR worldview in light of these biblical realities.

See Figure 6 on page 39: The Spiritual Nature of the World from Two Perspectives

The idea of a uniform spirit world sanctioned by God is a very persistent concept in the worldview of Africans with an ATR background. Christians often practice little discernment with regards to traditional methods because at the bottom of their hearts they still believe that all powers in the world are given by God and may be used if they are helpful. The first step in conversion from ATR to Christianity must certainly be a recognition of the Kingdom of Darkness at work in ATR followed by a categorical turning away from this false system towards the Kingdom of God. This is the repentance Paul spoke of when he entreated the idol worshippers of Athens, "In the past God overlooked such ignorance but now (that the Gospel has come) he commands all people everywhere to repent" (Acts 17:30). This repentance calls for a radical adjustment in one's worldview. If this adjustment is not fully made or is later called into question, the Christian will be ready prey for the deceptions of Satan as they come through the pervading practices in his culture.

b. God is remote and condemned man to a closed system dominated by lower spirits

In ATR God is perceived to be remote from man, not in a spatial sense, but in a relational sense. God is present everywhere but he is not available to man for the most part. He has placed man into a closed system of dealing with lower spirit beings without recourse to himself. Mediators to the various spirits are well known, but there is no effective mediator to God in ATR. God is not to be bothered with the daily affairs of men. Only after having exhausted all possible ways available to man through dealing with the spirits and mystical powers may one look to God with one's problem. Even then, it is more in fatalistic acceptance of what God has sent one's way than in the hope of eliciting his assistance.

This perception of a distant God and of man being condemned to help himself within a closed system dominated by lower spirits is graphically illustrated in the chart of *Figure 7 (see page 41)*.

Biblical Perspective: Kingdom of God	ATR Perspective: One God-ordained System	Biblical Perspective: Satan's Kingdom
A. SPIRIT BEINGS: *God:* Creator, Sustainer & Redeemer *Holy angels:* - angels in heaven - personal angels - territorial angels (at God's command; accept no worship; forbidden to worship)	*God:* Creator and detached Sustainer *Spirits/gods* involved in man's destiny: - tribal gods - village gods - family ancestors - personal gods	*Satan:* "god of this age" to pervert God's creation *Fallen angels/demons:* - powers of the air - territorial demons - personal demons (hiding behind false gods (I Cor. 10:20))
B. HUMAN LEVEL: -body, soul + spirit: spirit is the link to God but is fallen and separated from God -Holy Spirit restores link to God; empowers to do will of God; produces fruits and gifts of Spirit; prayer is access to power -true knowledge of God and worship -redemption means bonding to Christ: hope for now and future	-body + spirit: spirit links man to the supernatural power is drawn from super-natural by: -magic/sorcery -witchcraft -gifts from gods -ancestor cult -God is distant; religious activity revolves around spirits -cycle of bondage to spirits; no present deliverance from the system or ultimate hope	-body, soul + spirit are dominated by the flesh, world + devil -flesh + world is link to Satan + demons to produce the works of the flesh, demonization, demon possession and mystical powers -Satan hides behind false religion to deceive in areas of truth, power and deeds -bondage to Satan through fear of death (Heb.2:14); false hope through false worship/religion
C. REALM OF NATURE: -created + actively sustained by God -marred by sin; subjected to imperfections + Satan within limits set by God -man is forbidden to seek mystical powers in nature -God is sovereign in nature; he shields believers and turns all things for their good	-nature created by God but functioning of it delegated to lower spirit beings -controlled and disturbed by capricious spirits that man needs to appease -endowed with mystical powers given by God for man to use -man's aim is to help himself with the means "God put into nature" so that he will live the full span of his life as set by God	-Satan seeks full control of God's creation -Satan able to manipulate imperfections in nature -Satan can give powers to objects through demon attachments -Satan's aim is to use nature to destroy man or to keep him in bondage to his kingdom until death and hell

Figure 6: The Spiritual Nature of the World from Two Perspectives

Figure 7 presents how the Nso' people traditionally view sickness as to its cause, diagnosis and cure. The Nso' traditionally recognize six major categories of causes of sickness. All of these causes spring from relationships rather than from the realm of the physical. The question is never "what" but rather, "Who caused this sickness?". It may be a spirit being, a person using mystical powers, oneself or God. Whenever a sickness does not respond readily to normal rest and care the sick person or his relatives will suspect a supernatural cause. Investigations are then made to determine the agent causing the sickness and what reason he might have for giving the sickness. Diagnosis is typically by divination; the cure by some type of ritual to counteract whatever spiritual force is affecting the sick person. Ritual treatment is often accompanied by administration of traditional herbal medicines. However, medicines, whether traditional or Western, are not believed to be effective or to bring a permanent cure unless the right spiritual cause has been dealt with. If the sickness does not respond after the performance of one ritual, further investigations are made, and other rituals are tried along the possibilities listed in categories one to four of the above chart. If nothing helps one may ask himself whether the sickness is not self-caused through some transgression that needs confession. If that does not bring healing then, as a last resort, one may accept the sickness as the lot God has given. At this stage healing through rituals is no longer sought because there is no effective ritual to approach God himself.

The point is, from the ATR perspective there is always some hope as long as one is still dealing with the lower spirit world. The belief is that that there is an effective countermeasure in ATR against every kind of harassment from the spirit world. It is just a matter of finding the right one. But when dealing with God one is helpless. Thus, the ATR view of sickness constantly directs one back to the spirit world rather than to God, leading to ever increasing bondage to the system and the demonic influences behind it.

c. In ATR religion is man-centered

Man is at the center of ATR rather than God or any other spirit being for that matter. ATR is not so much a system of worship as it is a system of problem solving. Behind every ATR practice there is a human problem that man tries to solve by dealing with the supernatural. Spirits are appeased by offerings to keep them happy so that they won't bring "ill luck". They are entreated by sacrifices to "take their hands off" a person and stop bothering him. Men deal with gods to obtain riches and power. Mystical powers are sought for self-advancement, for protection against spirits and sorcerers, for power to rule and as a secret means to take revenge or to work out one's jealousy and envy.

Everything in ATR is defined from the perspective of man and how it

40

Cause	Diagnosis	Cure
1. Caused by an ancestor spirit		
a. to punish for breaking traditions	divination	-confession + sacrifice
b. ancestor manipulated by a sorcerer	divination	-sacrifice
c. ancestor seeking revenge	divination	-sacrifice
2. Caused by other people		
a. by putting sicknesses into body in form of objects	divination	-removing objects from body by magic
b. by witch visitations	self-diagnosis	-charms/moving away
c. curse by sorcerer	divination	-sorcerer lifting curse
3. Caused by gods/spirits		
a. personal god not recognized	divination	-recognition ritual
b. one's spirit stolen by a god	divination	-redeem one's spirit
c. evil god in area	divination	-chase god away
4. Caused by protective charms		
a. crossing charms/fetishes unknowingly	divination	-lifting curse by owner
b. interfering with items or places protected by charms	divination	-restitution and lifting of curse
5. Oneself is the cause "have my hand on it"	self-diagnosis	-confession by talking about it
6. Given by God	self-diagnosis	-accept it as fate

Figure 7: An African View of Sickness

serves him. This includes the concepts of "good" and "evil". "Good" is what is useful, helpful or sanctioned by society. "Evil" is what is not useful, destructive or anti-social. For example, the Nso' people traditionally recognize "good gods" and "evil gods". Both types can bring "ill luck". But when an "evil god" does so he may kill a person outright while a "good god" may only make a person sick and allow him to be redeemed through ritual. If the proper ritual is not performed he may still kill that person. Such a man-centered definition of good and evil is diametrically opposed to the Bible which defines good in light of the character and actions of a holy God, and evil as that which is in opposition to God.

     To summarize, this man-centered view of religion in ATR has fostered the following misconceptions: (1) that religion is there to serve man rather than

41

man serving God through it, and (2) that spiritual discernment is based on human judgment as to what is useful rather than on the holy character of God. The purpose of man in ATR is to do everything within his power to ensure that he will live a full life with many descendants, while the purpose for the Christian is to serve God and to glorify him. The Christian ideal can only be reached by discarding the man-centered view of religion coming from ATR.

d. In ATR God is not sovereign

ATR sees spirits at work everywhere. Spirit beings control much of nature. They are the real powers in control of the social and political domains of life. God, though he is the Creator, is less than sovereign in his creation. The spirits are perfectly capable of frustrating his purposes. God is perceived as having allotted to every man a full span of life, but the great fear of the traditional African is that he may die prematurely, cut off by some spiritual power before God's appointed time. This causes him to live in constant fear and in constant search of protection, never knowing who is ahead in the game, he or his secret adversary. There is no concept in ATR of the sovereignty of God over evil (Psalm 91) and of his ability to turn all things for good in the lives of those who trust him (Rom. 8:28). Often the ATR misconception that God is less than sovereign persists in the minds of Christians with the result that they live in constant fear of premature death and thus fall prey to Satan's devices.

5.0 Implications For Christian Communication and Counseling

As the Gospel has been communicated in the African context it has, in general, been readily received. Doubtless this was in part due to the fact that the African worldview is a spiritual one that overlaps substantially with the biblical view of the world and predisposes the traditional African favorably towards Christianity.

However, as we have shown earlier, the daily lives of African believers are often more controlled by fear of the spirit world than by security in Christ and trust in him. There is a marked tendency to revert back to traditional practices for protection against spirits and to make use of traditional spiritual powers in times of crisis. It is evident that some of the key misconceptions about God, man, and the spirits, that come out of the ATR worldview, are still very much a part of the worldview of many African Christians, even after several generations of Christianity, leading them astray and sapping the spiritual life of the Church. In this section we shall look at some of the factors that we believe have historically contributed to such a warped development of the Christian faith in Africa, and we shall suggest some strategies for Christian communication and counseling to counteract this tendency.

5.1 Some Factors Influencing the Response to the Gospel in Africa

a. Satanic strongholds in the worldview shaped by ATR

Satan has a number of powerful strongholds in the ATR worldview. Often not all of these are dealt with in the life of the believer or the church, allowing the devil and his demons to do their work of destruction behind the lines so to speak. These strongholds have already been mentioned in the preceding sections. Here we want to look at them from the perspective of the hold they have on the African. They can be seen as having a five-fold grip on the individual and on the society: a grip on the mind, on the emotions, on the will, on the society as a whole, and on people's desires and aspirations.

(1) *The grip on the mind* is established through Satan's deception in the area of truth about God, the spirits and man's relationship to them as outlined in the section dealing with misconceptions in ATR.

(2) Satan has *a grip on the emotions* through the overpowering fear of the spirit world which the ATR worldview produces in people. This fear is a powerful motivating force. If the new believer is not delivered from this fear it will drive him in times of crisis to make use of occult methods that he would not approve of at other times.

(3) Satan has *a grip on the will* through the clever system of bondage which ATR represents. ATR does not offer access to God in time of need. It constantly forces the person back to the system by using spirit powers against spirits, bringing the individual ever more under demonic influence.

(4) *The grip on the society as a whole* is established through the complete integration of ATR with social structures and functions. Relations to the family, the land and the tribe are all governed by rituals relating to ancestors and spirits, and so are many forms of social entertainment. Power to rule and to enforce the law rests on one's link to the spirit world and the amassing of mystical powers. Occult beliefs and practices serve as a binding force giving stability to the culture.

(5) *The grip on the desires and aspirations* is realized by the following powerful lures which ATR holds out to the individual:
- the lure of power and prestige
- the lure of secret methods for working out social tensions (revenge, anger, jealousies etc.)
- the lure of effective methods against spiritual attacks.

These lures represent strong temptations to the Christian, particularly if some of the other strongholds have not been completely destroyed in his life.

Spiritual warfare is fought on three fronts: the flesh, the world and the devil. The ATR worldview provides the devil with strongholds on all these fronts.

The flesh, consisting of the unregenerate mind, emotions and will, is in the grip of falsehood, fear and bondage. The world, the traditional society, is permeated with occult forces and practices. And lastly, ATR provides the devil with some very attractive baits to lure the individual further into his web. If the war is not fought on all these fronts in the effort to implant the gospel in the African setting, casualties are bound to mount.

b. The trap of the belief-gospel in Africa

As noted before, the fact that Christianity has spread so rapidly in Africa is in part due to the fact that the ATR worldview is able to accommodate quite readily at least some key elements of the gospel message. This has been a great opportunity for the spread of the gospel but also has been a dangerous trap. Receptivity is not necessarily true conversion, yet it is often mistaken as such, especially when the emphasis in the proclamation of the Gospel is heavily on believing in Christ as one's Savior from sin. To understand how this happens we need to look first at some of the functions of worldview in general and then at the ATR worldview in particular.

Worldview is the unconscious set of beliefs, assumptions, ideas and values that underlie a given culture. It consists of a set of perspectives for the different domains of reality such as the idea of self, the distinction of in-groups and out-groups, causes and powers in the universe, spatial and temporal orientation, and values and norms. They form a mental grid of what reality should be like. On the basis of this picture the group interprets the world around it and evaluates everything. New perceptions tend to be integrated into the existing picture of reality without changing underlying assumptions and values. Only on the basis of very strong evidence, such as experiential knowledge, will worldview perspectives change and give rise to new understanding. The principle we want to retain here is that the integrating function of worldview is stronger than the adaptational one.

In the previous sections we have shown that according to the ATR worldview the universe is governed by one unified hierarchy of spiritual powers, presided over by God. He rules the world through this system largely by delegation. Man's domain, the earth, is dominated by the lower spiritual powers and God does not normally interfere in this domain. He has provided man with intermediaries to the different spirit beings but there is no effective mediator to God himself, leaving an obvious gap in the system. This is where the message of Christ, as the Mediator to God, provides an answer to a deeply felt need.

Africans, therefore, respond quite readily to the call to believe in Christ as the way to God and to eternal life. However, such a response does not necessarily mean a complete shift of allegiance from the spirits to Christ. The ATR con-

44

cept of God not interfering in a spirit-dominated world does not yield readily unless there has been a definite experience of Christ's power over the spirits. The easiest way to interpret the Christian message through the grid of the ATR worldview is to see salvation and eternal life as something the Christian enters into only after death. Accepting Christ as Savior from sin now qualifies one for heaven to come, but does not necessarily change the conditions of life in this present world which is dominated by spirits. The result is dual allegiance. Allegiance to Christ now on earth as the one who will take us to heaven after death, while maintaining one's allegiance to the spirits for the needs and exigencies of this present life on earth.

c. The weakness of a Western gospel in the African context

One other factor that has often strengthened the trend towards dual allegiance and nominalism is that the gospel was introduced to Africa from the perspective of a foreign worldview and did not always address the felt needs of Africans.

The Gospel was brought to Africa by missionaries from Western countries. When they proclaimed the Gospel in Africa they often did so unconsciously from the perspective of their culture. Their brand of Christianity had been heavily affected by the prevailing Western worldview which is naturalistic and rationalistic. It has no room for spiritual causes in the universe. Things happen in accordance with definable laws of nature. Science and human ingenuity hold the answers to all of man's problems.

In this context Western Protestantism came to play down the supernatural and mystical elements of the faith such as the experience of miracles, spiritual gifts, and encounters with demons. Western Christianity developed a strong orientation towards analyzing the Christian message, systematizing its doctrines and discerning the truth. Faith is much more a response to knowledge of the truth than to a power encounter between God and the Kingdom of Darkness. The spirit world and the miraculous are recognized to be part of the biblical picture of reality but are downplayed as far as their relevance to the present age is concerned. Western evangelical Christians believe in miracles but do not really expect them to happen today. They believe in the existence of demons but, being ignorant of how demons work in Western culture, they have little practical experience with confronting them. As a result, they are skeptical when they hear about purported spirit activities and ascribe much of what they hear to superstition and ignorance on the part of those who report having those experiences.

It is this brand of Western knowledge-truth Christianity that came to encounter the spirit-oriented cultures of Africa. In these cultures, religion is concerned with tapping the powers of the spirit world in order to solve the problems of daily life rather than with the learning of theological truths. Anyone claiming to speak for God is first of all assumed to be a man of power. His words, though usually few, are weighty because of his personal intimacy with the powers of the spirit world.

In this setting, the Western gospel has been less than effective to produce a shift of allegiance from the spirits to the living Christ. There is often much emphasis on faith in Christ as the Savior from sin but little on his power to deliver from the harassment of the spirit world. Few churches practice deliverance ministries. Actions speak louder than words. Proclaiming Christ as deliverer without the practical experience of deliverance is not enough to change the core concept of ATR about the unbreakable grip of the spirit world on this life. At best it produces Christians with dual allegiance — allegiance to Christ for the hereafter while remaining bound to the proven methods of ATR for solving the problems of this life.

The Gospel provides for spiritual authority to confront the powers of evil, and holds out the promise of miracles to those who believe. The African by his worldview is predisposed to expect God to work in power, but the tragedy of the African church is that generations of church leaders have been trained in Westernized theological institutions to not expect God to work in power.

The ATR concept of an earth dominated by spirits in which God does not interfere is a very strong one. It is born out by a lot of experience and is unlikely to yield unless there has been at least some observation of Christ's power over the spirits, that is a power encounter of some sort such as the destruction of fetishes without harm to the believer or deliverance from demonic harassment in response to authoritative prayer. What is needed today is the liberation of the African church from the shackles of the Western gospel, so that it can fully assume its spiritual authority in Christ and minister in power to those in bondage to the Kingdom of Darkness.

5.2 Some Suggestions towards a Strategy for Christian Communication and Counseling in the African Context

a. Focus on Christ as author of the Kingdom of God

In the proclamation of the gospel more stress needs to be given to the power of the Kingdom of God over the Kingdom of Darkness. Christ, as the author of the Kingdom of God, came to destroy the works of the devil (1 John 3:8) and to redeem mankind from the Kingdom of Darkness and bring them into the Kingdom of Light (Acts 26:18). Some of the points to be stressed are the following:

- The existence of two kingdoms: the Kingdom of God or of Light (Mat. 12:25-28; 1 John 1:5,6; Luke 11:2) and the Kingdom of Satan or of Darkness (John 12:31, 14:30, 16:11; Eph. 2:1,2).
- Explain how the Kingdom of Darkness is manifested in the local culture in the areas of false worship, power and deeds.
- Satan's claim on man for his kingdom because of man's sin (rebellion against God) (Gen 3, Heb 2:14, 15).
- Christ, the Son of God, became man to bring the Kingdom of God to earth, the realm ruled by Satan and his spirits, and to open the way for man to enter the Kingdom of God (Mk. 1:14, Lk. 11:20, 17:21).
- The gospels show that Christ always has power over Satan and the demons/spirits (Mt. 12:29, Lk 9:1) because he is the Son of God. But as a man he still had to defeat Satan by his death for man.
- Christ died for man's sin to cancel any claim by the Kingdom of Darkness on all those who are "in Christ" (Col. 2:13,14).
- On the cross Christ defeated the Kingdom of Darkness as a man and for man by being completely obedient to God's will (John 14:30,31), thereby breaking the power of Satan over man. By his death on the cross Christ disarmed Satan and his demons/spirits and triumphed over them (Col 2:15) so that all in Christ can triumph over them as well (Heb. 2:14,15)

b. Encourage the practice of public renunciations of ties to the occult

In Africa the greatest deterrent to faith in Christ and to victory in the Christian life is fear of the spirit world. Release from this grip of fear often requires an encounter with the power of God as being greater than that of the spirits. One way to encourage such encounters is to encourage old and new believers to publicly renounce former involvement in occult practices and to destroy any objects related to these (protective rings, charms, fetishes etc.). As Christians claim their protection in Christ and take this step of obedience God will show them his power and advance his kingdom (Acts 19:18-20).

c. Encourage discernment by interpreting local manifestations of ATR from the biblical perspective

Often many topics of traditional African life and practices are taboo among Christians. Consequently Christians do not understand how Satan works through many of these traditional practices and come under demonic influence when they make use of them. The church should clearly explain to its people the biblical view of the spirit realm, especially of ancestor spirits, and relate this to the terms for spirits in the local language. One should avoid using borrowed terms for the biblical term "demon" but rather seek one or more terms from the local language. The Bible also uses several terms for demons. A borrowed term will not relate to the people's experience with the spirit realm in their own culture and will encourage the common belief that some of their spirits are not of demonic origin. In each culture the demonic manifests itself in different ways. The church should make a conscious effort to explain to their people each of the local manifestations from the biblical perspective and explain the spiritual consequences of entanglement with them.

d. Prepare the Church to deal with the demonic by teaching the biblical resources

African Christians know the power of the spirit world. Many live in the fear of spirit-induced disasters and premature death (c.f. Heb 2:14,15). They are all familiar with the traditional forms of protection and these constitute a constant temptation to them. The tragedy is that few church leaders teach believers the biblical basis for personal protection from spirits and how to minister to others under demonic attack. (See section 5.3 d. for some of the elements of spiritual warfare.)

e. Minister to the demonically oppressed

African Christians see spirits at work everywhere and readily suspect that they are being attacked by spirits. Whether these attacks are always real or not is besides the point. They are real to the person who perceives them, and he needs help. If the church does not offer help, the individual may be tempted to seek help through traditional methods, thereby now bringing himself definitely under demonic influence, if he was not to begin with. The point is that every church should seek to develop an appropriate ministry to those oppressed by spirits.

Special cells of Christians could be formed and trained to minister to these needs through authoritative prayer and social support. For example, if a person can't sleep because he feels harassed by spirits at night, the group might pray for him and teach him how to claim his protection and rebuke the spirits when he feels attacked. In addition, a member of the group could stay with that person each night to pray with him until he is free from the harassment.

Various helpful procedures have been developed by those who have extensively ministered to the demonically oppressed. Some of these procedures are quite involved and not easily applicable. However, no church should shy away from this ministry. It can start as a simple prayer group and be quite effective. The main point is that the group knows its position and authority in Christ and genuinely seeks the guidance of the Holy Spirit. In section 5.3 a simple procedure for such a spiritual warfare group is given.

f. Encourage the church to be open to all the gifts of the Holy Spirit and to expect God to work in power

The gifts of Holy Spirit are given to the church for its proper functioning, its own growth to maturity and its service to others (Eph. 4:12,13). Wherever there is a body of believers the Holy Spirit has given an adequate number of gifts to these believers to function in a healthy way. No local congregation will be what it should be, what Jesus prayed that it should be, what his Holy Spirit empowered it to be, until it understands spiritual gifts and encourages their expression (Rom 12, Eph 4, 1 Cor 12).

g. Encourage integration of the gospel with the everyday life of the local culture

As it has been shown ATR permeates all aspects of traditional life, giving Satan and his demons a powerful grip on society. To claim the society for Christ the church needs to beat Satan in his own game by inculturating the gospel into the very fabric of the society. The church needs to look at the functions ATR fulfills in society and develop biblical substitutes that are culturally appropriate to replace these ATR practices. (See M.G. Kraft 1978: Chapters 13-16).

For example, the concept of some type of extended family or lineage is at the core of most African societies. It serves many useful functions but it is generally held together by ancestral beliefs and rituals. The leader rules the family through his connection with the ancestors and ensures the protection of the family by amassing charms. Ancestor-oriented ritual is the glue that holds the family together. The question is how can a Christian leader rule the extended family on biblical principles and ensure family solidarity. Can the church develop a model for doing this in a way that is culturally appropriate and biblically sound? If this is not done families will continue to look to non-believers or compromising Christians to serve as family heads.

African life is full of ritual that provides structure and makes life meaningful such as rituals at birth, passage to adulthood, marriage, death, public crises such as drought, insect infestations, or plagues, house dedication, land transactions and other contracts, reconciliation rituals, cleansing from abominations such as incest, the agricultural cycle of seeding, hoeing, harvesting, etc. How can some of these be Christianized in order to make the Gospel meaningful to everyday life and fill it with worship of the true God? Often the church shies away from adapting indigenous ritual for fear of encouraging syncretism. It rather adopts foreign rituals. There are least two dangers in this: (1) that foreign rituals will not really satisfy the emotional needs of the people, leaving a felt need for the old ritual patterns to face everyday living, and (2) that the foreign ritual is misunderstood and wrongly applied, leading to a breakdown of useful structure in life.

An example of the first case is the sparse forms of death rituals that African churches have taken over from Western churches. Often these are very dissatisfying, leading the Christians to participate in traditional rituals based on ancestral beliefs. This shows that foreign Christian ritual that is not satisfying may encourage syncretism rather than discourage it.

An example of the second case is the Western marriage ritual which has been introduced to the Nso' and led to a breakdown in adequate marriage ritual among Christians. The Western type church marriage with white gown for the bride and a suit for the groom and attendants is very costly and difficult for the young couple to afford. It requires money and does not fit the patterns of contributions in kind that family members normally make to a traditional wedding ceremony. Thus, in Nso', young couples have tended to delay the church wedding ceremony until such a time when they are financially well enough established, which is usually after they started living together and often after they have had several children. This ambiguity with regards to the beginning point of the Christian marriage has contributed to a now common practice of trial marriage. A couple will start living together without a church wedding and later separate again if they do not have children or if other disagreements arise without this separation being considered a divorce. What is needed is a simple Christian wedding ceremony patterned on the traditional ritual of bringing the bride to the family of the groom before she moves into his house.

Integrating the gospel into the fabric of a culture is not something that can be legislated or invented. It is an organic process that happens over time as the Holy Spirit guides the believers to apply scriptural principles to their daily lives. However, this process heavily depends on two factors: (1) that the Scriptures are available to the people in their own language and (2) that the whole process is steered by leaders who are fully committed to the Scriptures and truly in touch with their culture and people's felt needs.

5.3 Some Suggestions for Conducting a Spiritual Warfare Group

a. The purpose of the group

The purpose of the group is for each member to train him/herself in spiritual warfare and to be available for counseling and prayer to those who feel oppressed by the demonic or live in fear of it.

It is recommended that each church have at least one group so that Christians under spiritual attack will know where to go for help and support. Once Christians learn to claim and experience their own freedom in Christ the church will be better equipped to engage in the objective level of spiritual warfare which is reaching others for Christ and breaking down satanic strongholds in their society.

b. The scope of ministry

Such a group will be confronted with a wide range of problems because in the African setting, many cases of sickness, personal misfortunes, interpersonal problems and natural disasters are seen as spiritual issues. The group needs to be constantly aware that there may be several sources to the problem of a counselee besides the supernatural source and that the counselee may need other help besides spiritual counsel and prayer. Other sources could be physical, social or psychological. However, dealing adequately with the spiritual dimension will, in many cases, be all that is needed. In others it will free the counselee from fear of the spirits and set the conditions under which other assistance can be fruitful.

A word of caution is in place here. In the case of acute illness the group should always direct the person to medical help after having put him under the protection of the blood of Christ against attacks from the demonic and after having prayed for his healing. If, after prayer, the counselee is still worried about demonic activity being directed against him the group should promise to continue to pray for his protection and possibly send some members with the counselee to support him in prayer during the medical treatment.

c. Composition and size of the group

Spiritual warfare is first of all fought on the subjective level, that is on the level of one's own personal life, before one can minister to others. Everything depends on the Holy Spirit. Unless we allow him to work in our lives we can't expect him to touch others through us. Therefore, every member of the group needs first of all to be committed to seeking and maintaining his own freedom from spiritual opposition, victory over sin, and a deeper life in prayer. This requires honesty before God and the members of the group as they pray for one another. To encourage this honesty among the members of the group and to put at ease those who come for help, it is best to keep the group small, maybe up to ten members.

There should always be a leader of the group chosen by the members. This function of leading meetings may rotate among several members as the group recognizes emerging leaders. As the group grows, and members learn to minister effectively, new groups should be formed around emerging leaders. These groups could be situated in different parts of the community in order to bring the ministry closer to the people.

d. Some elements and resources of spiritual warfare

The believer's security in Christ: The believer has been placed by God in Christ, received Christ's righteousness (1 Cor 1:30) and is fully acceptable to God. In Christ the believer is secure and the "Evil One" (the devil) cannot touch him (1 John 5:18). He cannot do any real harm to him because he can go no further than God permits him to go (Job 1:12; 2:6). The life of the child of God is not at the mercy of evil spirits. God is in control. He is stronger than Satan and any of his demons and their evil powers. God's children are safe in his love and no spirit can separate those who belong to Christ from the love of God (Rom. 8:38,39). He works all things in the life of his children for their good (Rom. 8:28) including any attacks by the evil powers.

The believer's victory and authority in Christ over spirits: As God has placed the believer in Christ he also has seated him with Christ on his heavenly throne (Eph. 1:3;2:6) where all spiritual powers are under Christ's feet (Eph. 1:21). The believer thus shares in Christ's authority over the spirits. In the name of Christ they are subject to him. On the cross Christ defeated them and disarmed them (Col. 2:15). They have no real power over those in Christ. The only weapon they have is deceit ("schemes of the devil" Eph. 6:11). They will threaten and harass the believer in order to make him fear and give way to them. But the believer is not helpless. He is the victor in Christ and has authority to rebuke them in the name of Jesus Christ and the power of his blood (Col. 2:10).

The concept of giving ground to Satan: The believer is safe from demonic influence as long as he remains in Christ and does not give ground to Satan. Moreau explains this as follows: "Demons can only influence believers to the extent that we allow them to do so. The act of giving or allowing Satan to take any amount of control in our life is referred to as "giving ground" (Moreau 1990:90). There are four main ways in which believers can give ground to the devil and his threatening spirits: through fear, involvement with the demonic/ATR, unconfessed sin, and through spiritual inactivity.

(i) *The ground of fear*: Fear is the most common ground. Fear is based on ignorance of the power of God and of our authority in Christ over spirits. If we fear Satan and his attacks through spirits he can easily trip us up, especially by making us seek protection through occult practices, thereby opening the door to demons.

(ii) *The ground of involvement in the occult*: Involvement in the occult (charms, fetishes, sorcery, divination, witchcraft, consulting ancestors and ritual to them, seeking gifts from gods/spirits etc.). God forbids all these practices (Deut. 18:9-13) because they are idolatry and lead the believer into fellowship with demons who are the powers behind these practices (1 Cor 10:20).

(iii) *The ground of unconfessed sin*: Every time we hide sin in our hearts without confessing it we give ground to the devil. Areas of special vulnerability are unforgiveness (2 Cor 2:10-11) and anger or grudges (Eph. 4:26-27). Sexual sins also thrive in secret and can become a ground for demons to influence us, leading us into the bondage of habitual sins. They defile the body which is meant to be the temple of God (1 Cor 6:18).

(iv) *The ground of spiritual passivity*: The believer who becomes spiritually inactive by neglecting the study of God's word, prayer and the fellowship with other believers opens himself up to deception by Satan and his demons. He will lack discernment and not recognize the schemes of the devil. He may open himself to spiritual guidance and gifts that he thinks are from God but, in reality, they are from demons.

The protection of the believer: A true knowledge of God, (his sovereignty over evil and his unchanging love for his children), and of one's position in Christ is the best protection against fear of the unseen forces of evil. Otherwise the believer's best line of defense against giving ground to the devil is a holy Spirit-filled life. Daily confession of sin is necessary to maintain a holy life. In addition we need to be alert to the devil's schemes (1 Pet. 5:8; Eph. 6:18), especially to those in our own culture, to pray always (Eph. 6:18), and to bring our thoughts under the control of Christ (2 Cor. 10:5; Rom. 12:1,2). By daily putting on the armor of God (Eph. 6:10-18) the believer chooses consciously to claim his position in Christ and to walk in accordance with it.

The weapons of the believer are (1) The Word of God (Eph. 6:17; Mat. 4:3-11) and (2) prayer in the Spirit (Eph. 6:18,19). These weapons are for beating back attacks by Satan and for breaking down demonic strongholds. Praying in the Spirit includes authoritative prayer which is not merely asking, but actually claiming for God territory that is held by Satan, binding Satan and his demons, rebuking them and casting them out in the name of Christ and the power of his blood. When under demonic attack the believer should not remain passive. He should claim his position in Christ, cover himself and his family by the blood of Christ and rebuke the evil forces. To cancel ground given to demons, the believer may need the help of mature Christians to confess his sin and to rebuke and bind Satan so that he will be free (James 5:16; Mat. 18:18-20).

The gift of discerning the spirits (1 Cor. 12:10). This is one of the gifts the Holy Spirit gives to the church for its ministry. It is the special ability to recognize evil spirits at work and to distinguish between the work of demons and that of the Holy Spirit. However, the ability of a group to minister to those oppressed by the demonic does not depend on the presence of this gift. Believers can exercise their authority in Christ over spirits without this gift, though they should always be open towards receiving it.

e. Meeting times of the group

The group should have a regular meeting at a specific time and place. However, each member of the group should be available to people in need at any time. People will feel freer to approach an individual with a problem than a whole group. The group member can then take the person to the next group meeting, or call together a few members to deal with this case immediately. Later on the case can be shared with the whole group for continued prayer and follow-up.

f. Suggested program for a group meeting

←   A time of worship and praise.
←   A time of personal heart searching and confession before God.
←   A time of sharing personal struggles and praying for one another.
←   A time of sharing, discussing and memorizing Scriptures relevant to spiritual warfare and walking in the Spirit.
←   A time of intercession for specific cases and of prayer against satanic strongholds in that community and in the country.
←   A time of counseling with and praying for people in need.

g. Suggested steps for the counseling and praying process

One member of the group should be clearly in charge of this process. He is the one who leads the discussion with the counselee and leads in prayer though he may invite the others to participate at certain times. Their role in general is to stay in the background and pray quietly throughout the whole process. They might pray against demonic interference, for the Holy Spirit to guide the leader, to illumine the understanding of the counselee, to convict where necessary, and to give words of knowledge to the group. At appropriate moments the leader will seek the counsel of the group members at which time they can share the insights the Holy Spirit has given them. If the group is rather large and intimidates the counselee the leader may take the counselee aside and do the interview with only one or two additional members present while the rest pray.

The following steps are very general guidelines. They are meant to especially help those who are engaging in this ministry for the first time in order to give them some helpful structure. We have tried to include what we believe are the essential elements in the process of ministering to those oppressed by the demonic and, at the same time, tried to keep it as simple as possible. These steps and the sample prayers should not be followed slavishly like a ritual. They are rather a point of departure for gaining personal experience. Each group needs to find its own style of ministry as the Holy Spirit leads them.

The steps below are based largely on the experience of James Abunaw of the Cameroon Association for Bible Translation (CABTAL) with spiritual warfare groups and on some points gathered from the following literature.

C.H. Kraft, in chapter 12 of his book Christianity with Power provides a simple procedure similar to the steps given below. A more extensive treatment of the subject from an African perspective is given by A.S. Moreau in The World of the Spirits, particularly in Chapter Six: Dealing with the Demonic. N.T. Anderson deals particularly with the topics of claiming one's identity in Christ and canceling grounds given to Satanic forces in the books and guides listed below. His booklet, Steps to Freedom in Christ, is a guide for taking the counselee through clearly written-out steps and prayers to cancel any ground he may have given to demonic forces and to claim his own freedom in Christ. This is a good guide to use with those who are well literate in English and have a good background knowledge of the Scriptures.

STEPS:

(1) *Give a short opening prayer*, inviting the Holy Spirit to come, to guide you into all truth, and to lead the time of ministry. Depending on the case you may also at this time want to bind any opposing spirit from hindering the counselee.

Sample prayer: Holy Spirit, come and take charge of this session. Show us what you want us to do and help us to cooperate with you in accomplishing your purpose here. In the name of Jesus Christ and the power of his blood, I take authority over every evil spirit and bind them from interfering at this time. I command peace and cooperation. Amen.

(2) *Interview the counselee.*

Sample questions: What would you like us to pray for? When did this condition start? What else was going on in your life when the condition started? Do you suspect any activity by spirits? Explain. This last question is important because many people will feel inhibited to talk about their fears of the supernatural unless they know they are taken seriously.

Listen to the counselee and constantly ask God to guide you to ask the right questions. If the counselee suspects involvement of the supernatural try to get a clear picture of his understanding as to the source: ancestor spirits, sorcery, curse, witchcraft, charms, covenants with gods and spirits, etc. Look for grounds that the counselee might have given to the devil for the demons to gain influence over him. If the counselee suspects someone behind these supernatural agents, ask about his relationship to that person. What happened between him and that person? Why does he fear that person? Do not go on too long. Decide on a tentative diagnosis and go on to the next step.

(3) *Explain briefly the theology of spiritual warfare*:
   a. The biblical view of the spirit realm based on the concept of two kingdoms.
   b. Christ's victory over the Kingdom of Darkness and the believer's position in Christ.

55

c. Concept of grounds. Ask the counselee if he is willing to take his stand with Christ in the Kingdom of God. Lead him in a prayer to claim his position in Christ.

(4) **Lead the counselee to cancel any ground he may have given to Satan**.

Instruct the counselee to expect mental opposition by Satan during this process. He will put thoughts of doubt into the counselee's mind such as, "This is not going to work," "Having charms is not a sin. God gave them for our protection". These are lies of Satan. Tell the counselee to share such thoughts as soon as they occur. Satan's power is in the lie. As soon as the lie is exposed the power is broken.

Lead the counselee in prayer to ask the Holy Spirit to reveal any unconfessed sin, especially in the following areas:

a. Relation to the occult: using charms, dabbling in sorcery, divination, covenants with spirits made by himself or by his parents, etc.

b. Relation to others: anger, unforgiveness (grudges)

c. Personal purity: lust, sexual sins

Lead the counselee in prayer to confess each sin and renounce any covenants and involvement with spirits. If charms are involved ask counselee to destroy them right then, or, if not possible right then, to do so later in the presence of others.

(5) **Pray for the counselee and his need.**

Put the counselee under the blood of Christ and claim Christ's protection over him. Take authority over spirits in the name of Christ. Also, pray for healing if sickness is involved. Bless the counselee in the name of Christ as is appropriate and as the Spirit leads you. Sample prayer: In the name of Jesus I bless you with: peace, forgiveness, confidence, release from worry, fear of spirits, or guilt. Other members of the group may also pray for the counselee and bless him.

Give the counselee relevant Scripture promises to claim. Also give him a short sample prayer to take authority over the spirits and rebuke them if he feels attacked again.

Sample prayers: In the name of Jesus Christ and the power of his blood I command you to leave! Or, I cover myself and my family with the blood of Jesus Christ. In the name of Jesus Christ I command you to leave!

(6) **Ask the counselee to go home** and claim the Scripture promises and exercise his authority in prayer. If there still seem to be unresolved sins ask him to continue to search his life before the Lord. Ask him to return after some time to share what the Lord has done. If the counselee is not yet ready to claim his own protection some members may visit him in his home for some time to pray with him.

56

(7) *The group continues to pray for the need*, claiming God's promises and seeking further guidance if necessary. It may also set aside a time of fasting in difficult cases.

(8) *When the counselee comes back* he should share what the Lord has done and any problems he may have encountered. The group members will also share anything the Lord has revealed to them. They should praise God for every sign of progress, even if it seems little. Then they should seek the mind of the Spirit as to the next step and continue to support the counselee in prayer and in practical ways.

6.0 Conclusion

The contents of this paper are largely based on personal observations made by the authors in Cameroon. Other sources have been consulted as cited in the bibliography. These sources have, by and large, confirmed that the picture the authors gained from Cameroon as to the ATR worldview and its effect on the church is quite similar across Africa. We are aware that this paper has many limitations, especially with regards to spiritual warfare in the African setting. Much needs to be learned in this area. In the end such learning can only come from the Holy Spirit as he leads God's people in personal spiritual warfare and ministry to others. If this paper has helped the reader to have a greater awareness of the nature of the spiritual battle in the African setting and stimulated him to become more active in spiritual warfare, then it has fulfilled its purpose.

Sources Cited in this Paper:

N.T. Anderson. 1990. The Bondage Breaker. Harvest House Publishers. Eugene, Oregon 97402, USA.

N.T. Anderson. Steps to Freedom. (13 pages) Freedom in Christ Ministries, 491 E. Lambert Rd., La Hara, CA 90631, USA.

R.J. Gehman. 1989. African Traditional Religion in Biblical Perspective. Kesho Publications: Kijabe, Kenya.

C.H. Kraft. 1989. Christianity with Power. Vine Books. Servant Publications. Ann Arbor, Michigan, USA.

M.G. Kraft. 1978. Worldview and the Communication of the Gospel. William Carey Library. Pasàdena, California, USA.

A.S. Moreau. 1990. The World of the Spirits - A Biblical Study in the African Context. Evangel Publishing House, Box 28963, Nairobi, Kenya.